For Walter and Molly

FOREWORD

One of my favorite artists is Jan Vermeer. There was a small print of his painting *The Maid with the Milk Jug* on the wall in a dark passage in my grandmother's house. It was part of the furniture so I took it for granted, but I never forgot it. I have included it here in this book of paintings.

I began to play "I Spy" with paintings with my own children when they were very young, and we had great fun choosing the paintings for our own I Spy Alphabet. As we looked into each picture, we found much that was familiar and a great deal that was unfamiliar. Often my children pointed out things which I had never noticed — an apple that had fallen to the floor, a funny-shaped shoe, the wind in the grass, a pattern on the carpet. They helped me to remember how to look and see and judge for myself.

Most art books live on the top shelf, out of reach, but this one is for the picture book shelf. It contains a handful of paintings for you to explore. I hope you will like them and have fun getting to know them.

Lucy Micklethwait, 1991

I SPY

—An Alphabet In Art—

Devised & selected by Lucy Micklethwait

A Mulberry Paperback Book, New York

I spy
with my little eye
something beginning with

Aa

René Magritte, *Son of Man*

I spy
with my little eye
something beginning with

Bb

Henri Rousseau, *Football Players*

I spy
with my little eye
something beginning with

Cc

William Hogarth, *The Graham Children*

I spy
with my little eye
something beginning with

Dd

Jan Van Eyck, *The Arnolfini Marriage*

I spy
with my little eye
something beginning with

Ee

Indian, *Workmen Building the Palace of Fatehpur Sikri*

I spy
with my little eye
something beginning with

Ff

I spy
with my little eye
something beginning with

Gg

Follower of Jan van Kessel, *Still Life with Fruit and Flowers*

I spy
with my little eye
something beginning with

Hh

Jean-Baptiste-Siméon Chardin, *The House of Cards*

I spy
with my little eye
something beginning with

Ii

I spy
with my little eye
something beginning with

Jj

Jan Vermeer, *The Maid with the Milk Jug*

I spy
with my little eye
something beginning with

Kk

Jan Steen, *The World Upside Down*

I spy
with my little eye
something beginning with

Ll

John Singer Sargent, *Carnation, Lily, Lily, Rose*

I spy
with my little eye
something beginning with

Mm

Francisco Goya, *Don Manuel Osorio Manrique de Zuñiga*

EL S.º D.ª MANVEL OSORIO MANRRIQVE D ZVÑIGA S ºD GINES NACIO EN Aº M·D·178

I spy
with my little eye
something beginning with

Nn

Jan van Huijsum, *Flowers in a Vase*

I spy
with my little eye
something beginning with

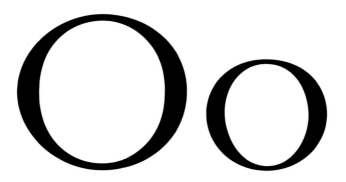

Henri Matisse, *Interior with Etruscan Vase*

I spy
with my little eye
something beginning with

Pp

Carlo Crivelli, *The Annunciation with St. Emidius*

I spy
with my little eye
something beginning with

Qq

Thomas Warrender, *Still Life*

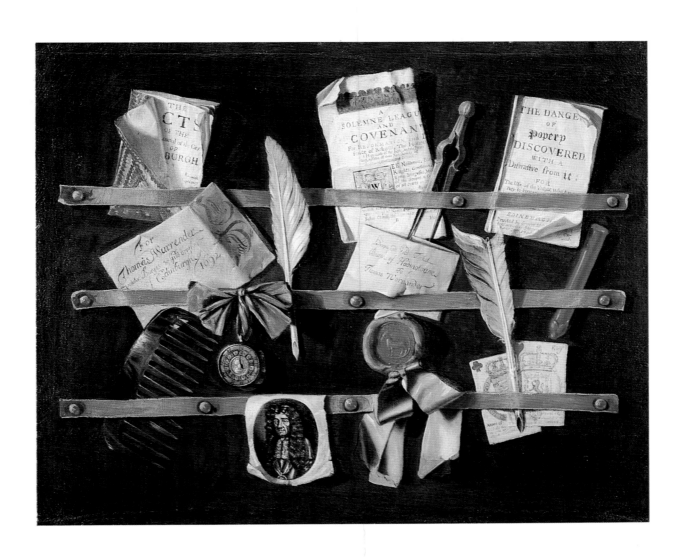

I spy
with my little eye
something beginning with

Rr

Marcus Gheeraerts the Younger, *Queen Elizabeth I*

I spy
with my little eye
something beginning with

Ss

Joan Miró, *Woman and Bird in the Moonlight*

I spy
with my little eye
something beginning with

Tt

Jacob Savery II, *The Animals Entering Noah's Ark*

I spy
with my little eye
something beginning with

Uu

Pierre Auguste Renoir, *Umbrellas*

I spy
with my little eye
something beginning with

Vv

Marc Chagall, *The Bride and Groom of the Eiffel Tower*

I spy
with my little eye
something beginning with

I spy
with my little eye
something ending with

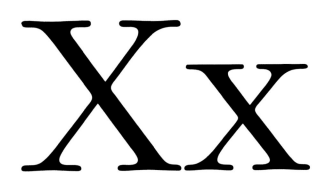

I spy
with my little eye
something beginning with

Yy

I spy
with my little eye
something beginning with

Zz

Wybrand de Geest, *Portrait of a Child*

I Spied with My Little Eye...

A apple
René Magritte (1898–1967),
Son of Man (1964)
Private Collection

B ball
Henri Rousseau (1844–1910),
Football Players (1908)
The Solomon R. Guggenheim Museum,
New York

C cat
William Hogarth (1697–1764),
The Graham Children (1742)
The National Gallery, London

D dog
Jan Van Eyck
(working 1422, died 1441),
The Arnolfini Marriage (1434)
The National Gallery, London

E elephants
Indian,
*Workmen Building the Palace
of Fatehpur Sikri* from
The Akbarnama (about 1590)
The Victoria and Albert Museum, London

F fish
Pablo Picasso (1881–1973),
*Sitting Woman with a
Fish Hat* (1942)
Stedelijk Museum, Amsterdam

G guinea pigs
Follower of Jan van Kessel
(1626–1679),
*Still Life with Fruit and
Flowers on a Table*
The Harold Samuel Collection,
Corporation of London

H heart
Jean-Baptiste-Siméon Chardin
(1699–1779),
The House of Cards (about 1735)
National Gallery of Art, Washington,
Andrew W. Mellon Collection

I inkwell
Sandro Botticelli (1445–1510),
Madonna of the Magnificat
(about 1482–1485)
The Uffizi Gallery, Florence

J jug
Jan Vermeer (1632–1675),
The Maid with the Milk Jug
(about 1660)
Rijksmuseum, Amsterdam

K key
Jan Steen (1626–1679),
The World Upside Down
(about 1663)
Kunsthistorisches Museum, Vienna

L lanterns
John Singer Sargent (1856–1925),
Carnation, Lily, Lily, Rose
(1885–1886)
The Tate Gallery, London

M magpie
Francisco Goya (1746–1828),
*Don Manuel Osorio Manrique
de Zuñiga* (born 1784)
The Metropolitan Museum of Art, New York,
Jules Bache Collection

N nest
Jan van Huijsum (1682–1749),
Flowers in a Vase (1726)
The Wallace Collection, London

O orange
Henri Matisse (1869–1954),
Interior with Etruscan Vase (1940)
The Cleveland Museum of Art,
Gift of the Hanna Fund

P peacock
Carlo Crivelli (working 1457–1493),
The Annunciation with St. Emidius
(1486)
The National Gallery, London

Q quills
Thomas Warrender
(working 1673–1713),
Still Life (about 1708)
The National Gallery of Scotland, Edinburgh

R roses
Marcus Gheeraerts the Younger
(1561/62–1635/36),
Queen Elizabeth I (about 1592)
National Portrait Gallery, London

S stars
Joan Miró (1893–1983),
*Woman and Bird in the
Moonlight* (1949)
The Tate Gallery, London

T turtles
Jacob Savery II (1593–after 1627),
The Animals Entering Noah's Ark
Private Collection

U umbrellas
Pierre Auguste Renoir (1841–1919),
Umbrellas (about 1884)
The National Gallery, London

V violin
Marc Chagall (1887–1985),
*The Bride and Groom of the
Eiffel Tower* (about 1939)
Musée National d'Art Moderne,
Centre Georges Pompidou, Paris

W water
David Hockney (born 1937),
A Bigger Splash (1967)
The Tate Gallery, London

X ox
The Limbourg Brothers (active 1411–16),
March from *Les Très Riches Heures
du Duc de Berry* (about 1415)
Musée Condé, Chantilly

Y yacht
Georges Seurat (1859–1891),
*Sunday Afternoon on the Island of
La Grande Jatte* (1884–1886)
The Art Institute of Chicago,
Helen Bartlett Memorial Collection

Z zigzag
Wybrand de Geest (1592–about 1660),
Portrait of a Child (1631)
Rijksmuseum, Amsterdam

*I would like to thank all the children, parents, teachers,
librarians, curators, and friends who have contributed
in some way or another and invariably with
enthusiasm to this I Spy Alphabet.*

ACKNOWLEDGMENTS

Pictures are reproduced by courtesy of the galleries and museums
listed on the preceding pages and of the following:
The Bridgeman Art Library (E, G, I, K, T);
Photographie Giraudon (jacket/cover, A); Photographie Giraudon/Bridgeman Art Library (X).

A Bigger Splash © D. Hockney 1967.
Pablo Picasso, *Sitting Woman with a Fish Hat*; René Magritte, *The Great War* © D.A.C.S. 1992.
René Magritte, *Son of Man*; Joan Miró, *Woman and Bird in the Moonlight*; Marc Chagall,
The Bride and Groom of the Eiffel Tower © A.D.A.G.P., Paris, and D.A.C.S., London 1992.
Henri Matisse, *Interior with Etruscan Vase* © Succession H. Matisse/D.A.C.S. 1992.

Cover picture: René Magritte, *The Great War* (1964), Private Collection.
Title page picture: Georges Seurat, *Sunday Afternoon on the Island of La Grande Jatte* (1884—1886),
The Art Institute of Chigago, Helen Bartlett Memorial Collection.

I Spy: An Alphabet in Art
Compilation and text copyright © 1992 by Lucy Micklethwait
The author asserts the moral right to be identified as the author of the work.
First published in Great Britain in 1992 by HarperCollins Publishers Ltd.
First published in the United States in 1992 by Greenwillow Books.
All rights reserved. Printed and bound in China
For information address HarperCollins Children's Books,
a division of HarperCollins Publishers, 195 Broadway, New York, NY 10007.
www.harpercollins.co.uk

20 HCUK 14

Library of Congress Cataloging-in-Publication Data
Micklethwait, Lucy.
I spy: an alphabet in art/devised and selected by Lucy Micklethwait.
p.   cm.
"Greenwillow Books."
Summary: Presents objects for the letters of the
alphabet through paintings by such artists as
Magritte, Picasso, Botticelli, and Vermeer.
ISBN 978-0-688-11679-8
ISBN 978-0-688-14730-3 (pbk.)
1. Painting—Themes, motives—Juvenile literature.
2. Alphabet in art—Juvenile literature.
[1. Art appreciation. 2. Alphabet.]   I. Title.
ND1146.M5 1992   759[E]—dc20
91-42212   CIP   AC